# DYNAMIC OPENERS & ENERGIZERS

## 101
## Tips and Tactics
## for Enlivening
## Your Training
## Classroom

■ ■ ■

By Bob Pike with Sara Anderson

 **Lakewood Publications**
A Maclean Hunter Company

## Quantity Sales

Most Lakewood books are available at special quantity discounts when purchased in bulk by companies, organizations and special-interest groups. Custom imprinting or excerpting can also be done to fit special needs. For details contact Lakewood Books.

■ ■ ■

## LAKEWOOD BOOKS

50 South Ninth Street
Minneapolis, MN 55402
(800) 707-7769 or (612) 333-0471
FAX (612) 340-4819

*Publisher:* Philip G. Jones
*Editors:* Bob Pike with Julie Tilka
*Production Editor:* Julie Tilka
*Production:* Carol Swanson and Pat Grawert
*Cover Designer:* Barb Betz, Betz Design

Contents of this book copyrighted ©1994 by Bob Pike and Lakewood Publications. All rights reserved. No part of this publication may be reproduced, stored in a retrieval system, or transmitted, in any form or by any means, electronic, mechanical, photocopying, recording or otherwise, without the prior written permission of the publisher. Printed in the United States of America.

10 9 8 7 6 5 4 3

Lakewood Publications, Inc. publishes *TRAINING Magazine; Training Directors' Forum Newsletter; Creative Training Techniques Newsletter; Technology For Learning Newsletter; Potentials In Marketing* Magazine, *Presentations* Magazine; and other business periodicals, books, research and conferences.

Bob Pike, Creative Training Techniques International, 7620 W. 78th St., Edina, MN 55439, (612) 829-1960, FAX (612) 829-0260.

ISBN 0-943210-64-X

# Contents

# Foreward

This book, *Dynamic Openers and Energizers*, is one in a series drawn from the best content of *Creative Training Techniques Newsletter*. The newsletter was conceived in 1988 by editor and internationally known trainer Bob Pike to be a one-stop resource of practical "how-tos" for trainers. The idea was (and still is) to provide timely tips, techniques, and strategies that help trainers with the special tasks they perform daily.

When the newsletter began, it was largely fueled by Bob's 20 years of experience in the field and by the best ideas shared by the trainers (more than 50,000 in all) who had attended his Creative Training Techniques seminars. As the newsletter grew in popularity, it also began to draw on ideas submitted by its readers. Today, the newsletter continues to search out creative approaches from the more than 200 seminars Bob and the other Creative Training Techniques trainers conduct every year and from the newsletter readers.

But no matter where the insights come from, the goal of the newsletter remains the same: To provide trainers a cafeteria of ideas they can quickly absorb, and then choose the ones that best suit their special needs.

This series of books represents the best ideas from *Creative Training Techniques Newsletter's* six years of publication. It is our hope we've created a valuable resource you'll come back to again and again to help address the unique challenges you face in your job daily.

Sincerely,
The Editors

# Introduction

**P**eople remember what we do first, best. That's why how we open a program is so important. Some people don't open a presentation at all, they just wander into it. Others use an icebreaker — it's fun, but there's no point. We want to create powerful openings that have people with us from the beginning. Consider these three things when choosing or creating any opening for yourself:

1. *Does it break preoccupation?* Does it get people mentally as well as physically in the room? Normally any opening that involves people, especially those that get them talking to each other — or accomplishing an activity will help do this.

2. *Does it facilitate networking?* Does it help people to get comfortable with one another? People may wonder: Can I contribute? Will I fit in? Do I know more — or less — than others here? When tension goes up, retention goes down. Once again involvement is the key.

3. *Is it revelant to the program?* I want everything that I do to make a point, to be relevant. This is especially true for my opening. If people remember first things best, I want them to remember that what we did right from the start was relevant. Whatever you do to open your program, make sure that it is relevant to the program, that it helps demonstrate why the program content is going to be useful for your group. It's a real plus if the opening also has an on-the-job application.

Another frequently overlooked area is the topic of energizers. There are times when you have heavy

7

content flow. People's minds are beginning to fog. You need to change the pace, but a break isn't appropriate. An energizer may be just the thing. A one- to three-minute activity that gives people a change of pace, a mental break, yet keeps the group focused. Energizers can also be appropriate when the group goes into a midafternoon slump.

This collection of the best of the *Creative Training Techniques Newsletter* provides you with resources in five areas:

1. Openers — to get your program off to the fastest possible start.

2. Meeting Your Peers — ideas to stimulate interaction when networking and improving lines of communication are important components of your program.

3. Energizers & Stress Relievers — for when your class needs a lift and change of pace.

4. Puzzles & Games — involvement activities that can energize and make a useful point, while fostering an atmosphere of light and wholesome competition.

5. Creative Resources — props, tools, and object lessons that can help drive home learning points.

In the final analysis, you must choose those ideas that will work for you and be relevant to the content. These resources, however, can make that task simpler.

*Bob Pike*

# Chapter One Tips: Openers

**B**ruce Handler, senior training specialist with the Federal Reserve Bank of Chicago, occasionally opens his programs by sitting in the audience and staying quiet. At class time he asks loudly, "Why am I sitting here?" This breaks preoccupation within the group since most have not realized he is the trainer.

The training point, Handler says, is that "I'm being innovative in how I open my session. You [as trainers] need to work smarter and look at the ways you have been doing things and make them better. We all need to be willing to change. We resist it, but its effect can be positive."

# 1

**Begin your sessions with innovation**

# 2

## Dream, nightmare cards stimulate discussion

Fran Collins, marketing administrator for the National Bank of South Carolina, uses "dream/nightmare" cards to open her classes. Each participant is given two index cards. They list their positive feelings about coming to training on the "dream" card and negative feelings on the "nightmare" card. No names are used.

The cards are collected, sorted into dreams and nightmares, and posted for participants to read on breaks. Collins says the exercise is humorous, stimulates conversation, and shows participants they are not alone in their feelings or thoughts.

**Descriptive name tents create trainee personality images**

Linda Kavois, a training specialist for Rockwell International, has found a way to energize participants, help them get acquainted, and at the same time gain clues she can use to more effectively deliver her training. She prepares piles of 3 x 5 inch slips of paper with single words on each — words like "creative," "aggressive," "practical," "analytical," "blunt," and "outgoing." Each of the piles has enough slips so that if all participants want to choose the same word, they can.

At the beginning of class, participants choose five words that describe themselves and staple the slips to their name tents. Then they share with the group or another person why they chose the words and why they created that image. The ice breaker also gives the trainer specific clues regarding how to deliver more effectively to each student.

# 4

**Pre-session mailings welcome attendees, enhance networking**

Karen Lynch, manager of sales training for Eveready Battery, makes trainees feel welcome by sending them a letter before classes begin with a reminder of how to get to the training center and the course starting time.

Attached to the letter is a name tag and one-half of a playing card. The personalized letter indicates the recipient will be asked the next morning to introduce to the rest of the group the person who has the other half of the card. This encourages participants to attempt to find each other that evening and also gets them to class early in order to meet the person they are to introduce.

**J**erry Conlin, a high school teacher, has a series of captionless cartoons mounted on cards. He places the captions separately on other cards, and as participants file into his training room, Conlin randomly distributes cartoons and captions. He then asks everyone to find the person with the correct corresponding caption or cartoon. The partners then conduct brief interviews and introduce each other to the group.

**5**

**Match cartoons, captions to speed introductions**

**6**

**Brief interviews reveal useful information about group**

Here's an ice breaker from Ed Jones of Management Training Consultants, Wakefield, RI, that is an excellent way to start a program when you have limited total class time.

Pair off your participants and allow them 10 minutes to interview each other, each person being interviewed for five minutes. They may talk about anything, but when they're done they must be prepared to share three things about the person they have interviewed:

1. Something unusual about their name.
2. Something they like about the person.
3. One thing the person wants to take away from the seminar.

There are a number of things about this ice breaker that will help warm up your group:

1. It's generally easier to talk about someone else than about yourself.
2. The introductions tend to be more complete.
3. Each person receives positive feedback at the beginning of the seminar.
4. You, the instructor, get some quick feedback about partici-pant expectations.

**N**ina Policastro, training director for the Junior League in Dix Hills, NY, gives each participant a small paper bag and then asks them to put three items from their wallet, briefcase or purse that show something about their personality or lifestyle inside the bag. In small groups of five or six, people then share why they selected the items. To make this opener more program-oriented, ask people to select three items that make statements about their jobs. If they're in customer service, for instance, ask them to select something that relates to how they help customers.

**7**

**Personal items reflect trainee personalities**

**8**

**Wild applause creates lively atmosphere**

When Ann Korb, a Brooklyn-based consultant, runs a training program for 12 or fewer people, she opens the session by having the group sit in a circle. Each person interviews the person on his or her left, asking name, company, job title, responsibility, and hobby. Then one person goes to the center of the circle and introduces the person he or she interviewed, ending with "I'd like you to meet…" That person then runs into the center of the room amid wild applause and introduces the next person while the first introducer sits down.

A creative question that generates lively discussion can be a great opener for a program. Tremain Michaud, a trainer for the Alberta Culture Board Development Program in Edmonton, starts presentations by asking people to discuss the question, "If you could meet anyone either living or dead, fictional or real, who would it be and why?"

An alternative Michaud uses: "If you could get five people in a room for a discussion, who would they be and what would you want to talk about?"

**9**

**Generate discussion with a creative question**

# 10

## 'Embarassing moment' stories spur spontaneity

Debbie Hoffman, director of marketing communications at the Sioux Empire United Way, pairs up attendees and gives them five minutes to find out the following information: name, company, hometown, and second most embarrassing moment. Each person then has exactly one minute to introduce his or her partner. She rings a bell at the end of the minute, and if the speaker isn't finished talking (usually in the middle of a very embarrassing story) the next person starts anyway. People who finish before the bell rings must remain standing until the minute is up.

This works as an ice breaker as well as a learning tool for making presentations in a specified amount of time.

Candace Kessler of the Illinois Prairie Girl Scouts suggests this ice breaker for a large group: Have participants who share birth months gather together. Give each group two minutes to make up a cheer or slogan for their month. Large groups should be broken into groups of five to seven — the best size to promote the interaction and participation of each person.

**11**

**Group-composed slogans promote participation**

# 12

**Futuristic scenario breaks figurative (and literal) ice**

Use this futuristic scenario as an ice breaker or point of departure in your courses, suggests W. Greg Lanier, Duke Power Co. training specialist:

"In the distant future, people begin to explore the galaxy and to colonize other planets. In view of the great distances and traveling times involved, colonists may be put in suspended animation for shipment. Some colonies receive more colonists than can be accommodated, so there will be warehouses full of frozen people, ready to be defrosted as needed...if ever.

"You are a colonist about to be put in cryogenic suspension. You are filling out a lengthy form in which all of your demographic and professional characteristics are listed. You come to a question that asks you to list up to six adjective-noun combinations (such as "hard worker" or "good parent") which describe you as a person. What would you list? What qualities do you have that would make someone else decide that you are worth thawing out?"

Have participants write out their list of six characteristics and then discuss them with each other. In larger classes, it is best done in small breakout groups; in small classes, a round robin works well.

**13**

**Having trainees act as one 'body' emphasizes teamwork**

Janet Bradly, human resource consultant with Work Cover, emphasizes working as a team, a body, or a group with this exercise.

Bradly gives each individual a card indicating what part of the body he or she is to represent: right leg, left leg, right arm, eyes, nose, etc. Then without speaking, participants must find the other people who are the same body part. Once that is accomplished they move to step three — find enough people to form a complete body, again without speaking.

Finally the body is whole and learns to walk, run, breathe, etc., and demonstrates the ability to do those tasks.

**14**

**'Key word' ice breaker focuses learner thought**

The "key word" ice breaker used by Terri Burchett of the Tucson Medical Center, Tucson, AZ, helps participants immediately begin thinking about the issues they will cover in the upcoming class. In preparing participant manuals for a class, she writes a key word related to the program material for each participant. For instance, for a class on participative management, she uses "listening," "empowerment," "feedback," "decision-making," etc. She slips a word into the back plastic cover of each participant's manual.

When participants arrive for the class, Burchett asks them to find their key words. In their one-minute introductions, which include giving their names, departments, and other information about themselves, they also must describe what their key words mean to them in relation to the course topic. Burchett often records their comments on a flip chart. The key words lead to discussion of the course content or objectives, and when posted can be reflected on throughout the course.

Lunch becomes a problem-solving exercise for small groups in multiday training sessions planned by Tim Huff, senior quality engineer for General Mills, Buffalo, NY. Huff has participants develop lunch menus on the first day of the course. Then after an opening mixer, the class breaks into small groups which are given budget information and a list of local "food sources," such as delicatessens, fast-food places, and restaurants. Each group plans lunch for a different day.

Huff says the activity challenges groups to analyze data and helps participants network. The greatest challenge, he says, is for groups to discover others' eating habits, likes and dislikes, diet restrictions, and to plan within budgets.

# 15

## Having small groups 'do lunch' promotes networking

# 16

**72-second opener gets attendees on their feet**

Seventy-two seconds is all participants get for introductions in courses led by Ann Verhaagen, sales trainer with Avon Products, Newark, DE.

After Verhaagen introduces herself, she tells participants they have 72 seconds to meet as many people as possible. She instructs them to tell others their name, where they live, and what company they are with. When time's up the class reconvenes.

This exercise, she says, gets participants on their feet and immediately involved in meeting others.

## M & M lottery elicits participant information

Introductions in Mary Slack's classes have a lottery-type feel to them. After participants share basic information, Slack, an organization and employee development specialist for Honeywell in Phoenix, AZ, asks them to take an M&M and answer a question according to the color they select. Here are a few:

Orange = If you could travel anywhere in the world where would you go, and why?

Red = What are three things you like to do in your spare time?

Green = What is something you've recently accomplished (on or off the job) that you're proud of?

Brown = If you had a completely free day how would you spend it?

Yellow = You just won $10 million. What is the first thing you would do?

# 18

**Warm-up makes a point about workplace diversity**

Gina Matkin, a training specialist with the Nebraska Department of Social Services in Lincoln, NE, uses an ice breaker that also makes a point about the value of workplace diversity. Participants sit at tables with four or five folders of a different color than the folders at other tables. The folders hold handouts and other information.

Before the workshop begins, Matkin tells participants to form work groups on their own. She asks them for input on what constitutes an effective work team. Answers typically vary from selecting team members with similar skills to selecting those with diverse skills.

She then tells participants each table's colored folders represent a unique skill. Keeping the folder they now have, participants are asked to form what they consider the best work group. Groups typically create tables representing all the folder colors.

The exercise introduces participants to one another, and Matkin points out that work groups of different colors, sexes, economic, and family backgrounds — working in harmony — can be the most productive because they bring different skills and perspectives to the table to solve problems.

Cathy Fleming, training manager for Hallmark Cards, uses well-known advertising slogans to help participants get to know one another. She leads the group in generating popular lines such as, "You deserve a break today," "Be all that you can be," and "Just do it," and writes phrases on a flip chart.

When the page is full, she asks attendees to add personal slogans to their nameplates and to share the meaning of those statements with the group.

The 10-minute opener allows everyone to get to know each other, Fleming says, but is not so personal that people are unwilling to share. Some even keep their nameplates to display in their offices, she says.

## 19

## Ad slogans foster group introductions

# 20

## Relating dissimilar objects taps creativity

At the outset of Sharon Johnston's unit on problem-solving, participants are encouraged to use their thinking skills on a new level by trying to find similarities between two completely unrelated objects. Johnston, a training specialist with Prudential Home Mortgage in Minneapolis, uses a prepared list of pairs of dissimilar items — such as, "a beaver's dam and a typewriter" or "customer service and groceries" — to force attendees to view existing objects (and ultimately, problems that need to be solved) in a more creative fashion.

# Chapter Two Tips:
# Meeting Your Peers

**21**

**Simple graphic displays familiarize trainees**

This session opener puts trainee backgrounds in the forefront to help familiarize a group.

The opener involves creating a "name tent" on a sheet of paper or card stock folded to stand like a small tent. Have people interview one another in pairs. While they interview, have them create the following on the name tent:

**1.** My partner's name as she or he would like to be called (large letters, in the center).

**2.** My partner's organization (smaller, upper left).

**3.** My partner's primary goal for the course (smaller, upper right).

**4.** What would make the course a success for my partner (smaller, lower right).

**5.** What would make the course a disaster for my partner (smaller, lower left).

The information can be summarized as an introduction in groups of six if the class is larger (20 or more) or the length of the course is short (less than three hours). Otherwise you may want to use paired introductions of less than one minute each for all the participants.

**H**ere's an effective opener that can be used in a variety of forms to promote interaction.

Have participants complete any five of the following:

1. The department I work in ____.
2. My three all-time, favorite movies are ____.
3. In high school I was considered ____.
4. Outside work I'm good at ____.
5. My favorite food is ____.
6. My favorite fiction book is ____.
7. My favorite nonfiction book is ____.
8. The best part of my job is ____.
9. The worst part of my job is ____.
10. The best supervisor I ever had was ____ and here's why: ____.

Place people in groups of five to seven. Have each person select a question, and share his or her answer. Since not everyone will have answered each question, this creates some spontaneity. Have participants stand and share the most interesting things they learned about the person to their left — if group size is not prohibitive — which will provide introductions of everyone in the room.

Wrap up by asking each table to select one phrase they'd like you, the trainer, to complete.

**22**

**Short-answer activity promotes interaction**

**23**

**Let learner input guide your training approach**

If you ask your participants to introduce themselves and recount their previous training experiences, you provide a focus for their introduction, and they provide you with information that offers insight into the kind of training style they favor, as well as their level of expertise.

When training experienced participants, Frank McCowatt, a training and development specialist for Canada Wire and Cable Ltd., has them describe similar training programs they've participated in — focusing on style of delivery and what they liked/disliked about it.

That helps McCowatt recognize participant's previous involvement, and secondly, allows him to assess the group's, as well as individuals', topic "maturity." It also gives him ideas as to how he might best approach that particular group.

**Sharing personal facts builds group trust**

This ice breaker is tailored to a group of 15 to 20 people that work together and feel they know each other well. Each participant is asked to write one personal fact about themselves they think no one in the group knows. Then, as the seminar leader reads aloud each fact, every person in the room writes down the name of the person to whom they think the fact relates.

Reread each fact one at a time and have people call out names before the participant confesses. Each person should keep track of how many correct guesses they make. It's a fun activity that also clearly demonstrates to participants how quick we are to prejudge people.

Consider adding a stipulation: The fact participants write about themselves should be true only for them and no one else in the group. People will be surprised to find how many things they thought unique to themselves are shared by many in the group.

**25**

**Group writing fosters teamwork**

Here's an ice breaker to use with groups heavy with trainees resistant to activities sometimes considered frivolous or too personal (such as imitating tubas playing "Twinkle Twinkle Little Star" or sharing childhood secrets.

• Divide your group (25 or fewer people) into two teams. Tape a large flip-chart page to the wall for each team. Give each team a marker, and have the members form a line about 10 feet from the paper.

• Instruct each team to construct a complete sentence on the flip-chart sheet, written one word at a time — with each team member writing one and then passing the marker to the next person in line — until the page contains a sentence complete with subjects, verbs, and punctuation. No preplanning of sentences is allowed, and team members cannot insert words between words already on the page. Each member must contribute at least one word, and the rotation should continue until the team completes a sentence.

• Designate a prize for the winning team before you begin the exercise and make a presentation after reading out loud the sentences completed by each group.

• If appropriate to your training, this exercise also is a good starting

point for discussion about teamwork and observing, analyzing, and
thinking ahead.

Two variations to consider:
Require that each word in the
sentences begin with a specific
letter, or have the teams compete
one at a time against the clock so
the other team (or teams) can
observe the interaction.

# 26

## Switching name tags enlivens conversation

This exercise is designed for participants who know each other, or maybe just think they know each other. Joe Hanson, manager of human resources planning for Navistar, has participants write four adjectives that describe themselves on name tags, which he then collects and randomly redistributes so each participant wears the description of another person.

Throughout the day people read the adjectives and try to guess which participant the words describe. At the end of the day, people check their perceptions as everyone gets a chance in a large-group setting to guess who fits each set of adjectives.

**27**

**Question prompt cards urge discussion**

This ice breaker not only helps participants introduce themselves, but also gets them thinking about the focus of your training program. Barbara Herd at Cablevision Systems uses it in a program on the "Role of the Supervisor," but it can easily be adapted to other courses.

The session begins by placing a stack of 3 x 5 inch cards in the center of each table (assuming you're using small groups of five to seven people). Each card has one question on it. Each participant picks a card, reads it aloud, and then completes the partial sentence. Some of the sentences that prompt discussion as well as introductions: "The best pet I ever had....," and, "The thing I learned later that I wish I'd known sooner was...."

**28**

## Looking goofy, laughing warms up crowd

Everyone is asked to look silly during the introductions of trainer Gary Kebschull's programs. All participants, and Kebschull, fold newspapers into paper hats that they wear while introducing themselves to the class. Kebschull makes the point that "We're all in this together, and because we are going to take some risks, we may look goofy at some point. We don't have to anxiously wait for that moment to happen; it is happening right now." He says it is like telling participants to swallow a live frog first thing in the morning—nothing worse can happen that day.

**H**ere's an effective way to divide participants into small groups and at the same time gauge the experience levels that exist in the group. Divide participants into two groups and have one form a circle facing inward, the other form a circle inside the first circle facing outward so each person looks at a partner.

Tell the outer group to move clockwise and the inner group to move counterclockwise until you tell them to stop. Have the people directly facing each other spend a few minutes talking about their previous jobs and how those positions prepared them for their current positions.

That information is then used for everyone to introduce their partners to the rest of the group. Clusters of partners can form the work groups for the next part of the class.

**29**

**Creative grouping activity gauges experience levels**

**30**

**Group learners according to their interests**

Dave Dahlen, a park ranger with the National Park Service, helps participants get acquainted by asking a series of questions which reveal individual interests. For example, "I enjoy: A. classical, B. jazz, C. soul, D. rock music." Once each person has made a choice, participants divide up into groups with similar musical tastes. After a short get-acquainted period, another question is asked, such as, "I enjoy Italian, Chinese, American, or French cooking." The groups then change, based on those answers, and another short discussion period takes place.

At the outset of classes, Charlene Walter, director of training at the Sheraton Hotel Long Beach, asks participants to state their name, company or department, and a specific favorite food. She tries to remember all three, and periodically throughout the course goes around the room to review. At the end of the course, she asks the group upon questioning to answer either name, food, or job for specific individuals. She asks someone to volunteer to provide that information for one row or one table, and then asks one individual to try it for everyone.

**31**

Knowing attendees' favorite foods enhances name recall

**32**

**Mixing trainees by geographic area breaks up cliques**

To ensure that participants from a variety of locations mix with people from other regions, Ray Elliott of the New York State Department of Labor organizes small groups prior to his classes. Elliott reviews the roster by geographic area, and makes an effort to put one trainee from a particular area per table.

He then posts the groups on flip-chart paper and tapes assignments on the wall near the tables where he wants the groups to sit. Elliott says the strategy enables participants to begin networking before class starts and breaks up cliques.

**A** "show and tell" session at the beginning of or during a training session helps participants get acquainted and gives the instructor insights into attendee concerns, says Patty Couch, sales information systems analyst for Hallmark Cards, Kansas City, MO. Her participants share a problem they hope to resolve using the training being given, an accomplishment from another training class, or something related to the course they'd like to share.

**33**

'Show and tell' session reveals learner concerns

# 34

## Test attendees' ability to fib with personal facts

Testing participants' ability to fib can help trainees get acquainted, says John Tierney, director of staff development for the State of Connecticut. Tierney has a group of trainees unfamiliar with each other break into pairs, then asks attendees to write four personal facts about themselves, three that are true and one that's completely false. Partners exchange lists, then try to guess which "fact" is the false one.

In addition to being an ice breaker, this exercise can serve as a jumping-off point for a discussion about judgments and misconceptions by the entire class, Tierney says. For example, with small groups, rather than having trainees pair up, have participants write their four "facts" on a flip chart and have everyone record their individual guesses.

In a program for newly promoted assistant managers, M. Shane Moran, regional training manager, Pep Boys, Philadelphia, gives participants a blank page with "Top Dog News! Who's Who in the Business World" printed at the top. Moran asks participants to write a newspaper-style article announcing their promotion and citing reasons why they deserved the promotion.

Participants then share their articles in small groups. As they talk, each group uses a sheet of flip-chart paper to write five common reasons its members were promoted. The result, when the pages are posted, is a list of the qualities of a good supervisor — Moran's first topic of the day.

## 35

**'Promotion notices' activity lists desirable manager skills**

# 36

**Product, commercial slogans pair learners quickly**

Vickie Steffan, a trainer with Blue Cross Blue Sheld of Virginia, Roanoke, VA, uses product/commercial slogans as a way to break a group into pairs for activities. Steffan writes part of a commercial slogan on a card and puts the second half of the slogan on another card.

For example, on card 1 she puts, "Plop, plop, fizz, fizz..." and on card 2, "Oh, what a relief it is." She hands out the cards and asks participants to find their partners.

**A**s an opener and to facilitate networking among participants in large groups, Anne Robinson, consultant in human resource development with Creativity, Communication, Common Sense in Austin, TX, hands each arriving participant a slip of paper with the words, "All Aboard the I Train!" on it. The slip also bears the name of a city plus a list of train parts and personnel, such as engine, passenger car, observation car, pullman, diner, caboose, engineer, fireman, brakeman, conductor, with the number of parts and personnel matching the number of people to be in each small group.

Each slip has one type of car or personnel checked. Robinson encourages participants to look for the rest of the "train" and "crew" headed for the same city (tables are labeled for each of the given cities). When the groups assemble at their tables, people introduce themselves and tell the small group the most exciting/interesting tip, technique, or method they have used concerning the topic of the course.

**37**

**Assembling trainees as parts of a train promotes interaction**

**38**

**Personal lifelines provide weightier introductions**

Michael Mezack, director of continuing education and associate professor of educational psychology and leadership at Texas Tech University, Lubbock, TX, uses "personal lifelines" to help attendees at his sessions get to know one another beyond name and job title.

Each trainee draws a line on a piece of paper (or several pieces, if necessary) representing his or her life to date. At the far left end, participants fill in their year of birth. The other end is marked with the present date.

Participants then mark important life events along that line — personal, professional, or simply interesting — with an eye toward illustrating what brought them to where they are today.

Next they take turns explaining their lifelines to the group. It may be wise to set a limit of several minutes per person if time is a factor, Mezack says. Students may post their charts on classroom walls for others to review at their leisure.

Mezack displays and explains his own lifeline, making it clear that people may be as candid or reserved as is comfortable. The technique is especially useful in smaller groups, as explaining the lifelines can take several minutes per participant.

**T**his ice breaker by Betty Hertz builds a group's self-esteem and fosters bonds among trainees.

Hertz, a consultant for Windemere Consultants, Anchorage, AK, divides participants into groups of at least six and asks them to compose a "group résumé" to publicize their group's talents and experiences. Hertz chooses a job for the groups to apply for, and gives each group markers and a sheet of flip-chart paper to display their résumés.

She tells them to include data that sells the group as a whole, such as educational backgrounds, total years of professional experience, positions held, talents, major accomplishments, etc. Each group shares its résumé, and the class celebrates the resources of the entire group.

**39**

## Group résumés build esteem, foster bonding

**40**

**Vanity license plates acquaint, entertain learners**

At the beginning of her sessions, Jeanine Dederich, training manager of Associated Bank, Menomonee Falls, WI, gives each participant a form designed in the likeness of a blank license plate, and asks them to create their own personalized plates, using no more than seven letters or numbers.

She then asks participants to introduce themselves to the rest of the group using their new "vanity" plate as a starting point. She asks each participant to give the group a few moments to "decode" the plate before explaining it, as some can be fairly tricky.

Sample ideas are: SLSMN = salesman; WKGMOM = working mom; DADOV3 = dad of three; INVSTR = investor; H2OSKER = water skier.

# Chapter Three Tips:
# Energizers & Stress Relievers

# 41

**Divide attendees into groups with simple melodies**

Jo Ann Birkner, director of training and development, Tarrant County Junior College District, Fort Worth, TX, offers this activity as an ice breaker and a way to divide participants into small groups.

Have everyone in your session draw a slip of paper from a container. Each slip should have the words of children's songs or nursery rhymes with familiar melodies: "Three Blind Mice," for example.

Carefully prepare by using as many song and rhyme titles as the number of groups you desire and as many slips with each individual song as the number of participants within each group.

For groups of six, for example, create six slips with the name of one song. When everyone has drawn their "secret saying" have the participants find the members of their small group by singing their song as they move about the room.

Stop when most have found their group. Have any unclaimed souls sing their song and be claimed by a group.

**42**

**Solicit learners' jokes to energize group**

Humor and audience participation are great class energizers. To make both a part of your next seminar, take time at the beginning to ask for volunteers who know a good joke and will agree to tell it. List their names on flip-chart paper and post the list. Let participants know that throughout the afternoon, for instance, anytime they feel a need for an energizer they should say, "I think it's time for a good joke." That person then selects someone from the flip-chart list to tell a joke.

The joke may not be particularly good, but it serves as an effective energizer, participants enjoy it, and it also gives a brief break. You might want to ask your group to stand while the joke is being told; that gives the additional benefit of a controlled stretch break.

## 43

## Group-answered questions reinforce learning

This ice breaker can be used in a number of places during a training program. Consider using it when you want to rearrange groups, reinforce learning, or have trainees develop questions.

Assume you have 25 participants, seated five to a table. Ask each person to walk to the nearest wall, and then form groups of three, containing not more than one person from their previous groups. Once the groups are formed, each discusses their response to a question, such as: *What's the most useful thing you've learned so far? What one question would you most like answered?*

You now have a choice. If you've asked participants to generate questions, you can go from group to group while they're still standing and have the other groups answer the questions, or answer them yourself. The second choice is to have participants reassemble in new groups of five, with no more than two people from their previous groups. If they're sharing lessons learned, each person shares an important lesson learned related by someone else in the group from which they've just arrived. Or if there have been questions generated in the previous group, the new group will explore the answers. The new groups can then stay together when returning to the tables.

Group size is flexible. The exercise offers the advantage of group interaction and the sharing of valuable — and sometimes not so valuable — experiences. It takes roughly five or 10 minutes and provides a controlled stretch break.

**44**

**Toys inspire trainee relaxation, creativity**

Karen Vetrone uses a variety of toys in her training sessions because she believes learning best takes place in a relaxed, positive atmosphere. She encourages her trainees to handle the toys, ponder perspectives, allow their minds to wander, and consider new ideas as they relax.

Her favorites props include Space Tubes (clear plastic tubes full of mesmerizing, slowly floating stars, moons, and sequins), octoscopes (like kaleidoscopes, except they show eight triangles of whatever they're pointed at), and "Koosh" balls (like rubber pompons).

"I refer to the toys in my introduction," she says. " The tube is like the mind, full of potential when at rest, amazingly rich when it is turned around by new ideas. In each seminar, we will be like octoscopes, seeing things from many different perspectives." And the Koosh ball, she says, is great for creation of metaphors: "Working as a trainer is like the Koosh ball because..."

During a recent management skills workshop, one of her manager trainees reported this reaction: "You know, I thought at first these would be distracting...but I watched the other participants playing with them as they thought and spoke. I went out and bought a Koosh ball and put it on my desk. Now, when someone comes into my office, I can tell a lot about what's going on with them just by the way they play with the ball."

Vetrone's testimonial: "Yes, I travel a lot, and yes, I try to always limit myself to carry-on luggage. And yes, my toys always come with me."

**45**

**Startle tactic refocuses attendee focus**

Rae Brury, a northern region trainer for the state of California, gets her participants' attention in a novel way. She begins her class by placing a glass of water on the table next to her — a typical arrangement that doesn't attract notice. But if she sees members of the class starting to look as though their minds are wandering, she picks up the glass and slowly begins pouring the water onto a prearranged cloth or dish as she continues to talk.

She relates the time it takes to empty the glass to the material at hand. For example, "In the time it takes to empty this glass, a million dollars worth of unemployment insurance claims have been filed." The technique proves to refocus class attention on the lesson at hand.

**46**

**Chocolate chip cookies are 'never fail' motivators**

C hocolate chip cookies are, arguably, the ultimate classroom motivator. Here's how Lauren Irwin, training manager for FAA Credit Union, uses that idea during class:

Irwin places several slips of paper in a bowl, each listing an ingredient to a recipe for chocolate chip cookies. When participants answer questions correctly, they take an ingredient slip out of the bowl and pin it to a posted picture of a chocolate chip cookie. When a group answers enough questions to empty the bowl and complete the recipe, Irwin brings out a large tray of cookies as a reward.

**47**

**What goes around, comes around**

Robin Ruhf, a training consultant for Southeast Regional Center for Drugfree Schools and Communities in Atlanta, uses indoor boomerangs (small lightweight boomerangs made of balsa wood) to demonstrate an important point in her material.

When she throws the boomerang it circles and returns to her — an illustration of the idea that even though we often think the little things we do aren't going to affect us, inevitably they do return to have an impact on our lives and those in our surroundings.

**48**

**Brainstorm activity offers clues to a group's motivation**

Steven Wright, a development manager for IBM Canada, opens his classes by posing this scenario: Imagine it is a Friday afternoon, 96 degrees outside, and there's a big party scheduled after class. The class is not excited about the subject before them, yet it's the most critical point of the training program. How do you get them to pay attention?

Wright allows the participants three to five minutes in small groups to come up with their solutions. As they share ideas, he picks up keys to their motivation that he can use to make his classes more productive and energizing.

# 49

## Visualizing exercise relieves stress

After a visualization exercise in her stress-management class, Georgia Cortez, trainer with the Gas Company of New Mexico, hands out paper and crayons or markers and has participants draw pictures of the peaceful scenes they have just imagined.

Cortez says their artistic efforts are a way for participants to communicate to themselves about the feelings they have just experienced.

They can later hang their work in their offices or homes as reminders when they are tense and stressed that they have a "special place" to go to relax.

**P**aper airplanes flying around a seminar room might seem like an odd way to end a session, but Sue Mack Gaulke, president of Successworks, encourages it.

She gives attendees a blank piece of paper on which to write their names and telephone numbers. She then asks them to make the sheets into paper airplanes. When she gives the signal, they zip the planes around the room. All participants are asked to catch or find someone else's plane.

Each participant is then asked to telephone the person whose plane they caught two weeks after the workshop to discuss how they have applied the new skills they learned in the session.

# 50

## Paper airplanes foster post-session networking

# 51

## Posting 'warm fuzzies' builds learners' self-esteem

This "warm fuzzy" exercise can build self-esteem and help members of a small class be more attentive to others in the group. Marilyn Moen, director of training at Moen Training and Associates, posts flip-chart sheets with each participant's name at the top around the room. Throughout the seminar, each person should write one sincere compliment or a description such as "enthusiastic" on each person's sheet.

Janet Bradly, a human resource consultant with Work Cover in South Australia, enlivens potentially dull material by analyzing it for a key word and then assigning an action to it. Every time that word is mentioned during the session, the group must perform the action, which might be a cheer, a boo, or a clap. The actions also help burn those concepts into trainees' memories.

Though your class might start to sound like the audiences at screenings of *The Rocky Horror Picture Show* or your kids when they watch *Sesame Street*, the aim is to keep concentration and interest high, and to get the group to focus on key words, ideas, and attitudes.

Bradly says you might consider having an assistant hold up cue cards — like the "applause" sign used in television studio audiences — to help participants recognize their cues.

**52**

**Claps, cheers enliven dull material**

# 53

**Play-Doh exercise shows trainers how they 'sculpt' workforce**

During a train-the-trainer presentation for the Florida Department of Highway Safety and Motor Vehicles, trainer Rene Starnes emphasizes that trainers mold, shape, and design the workforce of tomorrow by the quality training programs they present today.

The presentation begins with a discussion of some of the intangible qualities that transform a mediocre trainer into an excellent trainer. The qualities are listed on a flip chart. Participants are then asked to choose the quality from that list which they would most like to have. At that point, Starnes passes out Play-Doh and asks that they turn that important intangible quality into a tangible product, a sculpture of some sort which will represent that quality.

Starnes says the group can be initially skeptical, but has fun once they begin molding the sculptures. Creativity is unlimited. Participants exhibit their creations and explain their meanings. In one case, a participant made a flower pot with buds poking up and related it to training by saying the flowers were program participants who would develop and grow from the nurturing and empathy of the trainer during the session.

Starnes presents to the class this adage from ancient philosopher Confucius, "If you tell me, I may listen; if you show me, I may understand; if you involve me, I'll learn."

Participants are able to relate the importance of experiential learning to the Play-Doh session and the program ends up being informative as well as fun, says Starnes.

**54**

## Using puppets in role-plays reduces tension

Simple puppets made by participants help relieve the tension role-playing might elicit in seminars led by Janis Miller, manager of education for Southwestern Bell in Kansas City, MO. Miller supplies white socks, yarn for hair, double-sided tape, safety pins, and markers. She has each student draw a face on a sock and add yarn hair, mustaches, beards, etc. to make a puppet.

Miller says preparing the puppets reduces tension and anxiety. The puppets make role-playing easier, too, she says, because students can direct attention to the other person's puppet as they act their roles.

To break the ice in her classes, Jan McKean, church ministries director with SDA Church, Manukau City, Auckland, New Zealand, passes out a humorous drawing that represents the different stages of life. McKean then asks participants these questions:

• Which figure best represents where you are now in life?

• Which figure would you like to be and why?

• What three things would you like to see take place as a result of this seminar?

She breaks the class into small groups and has participants discuss the first two answers. The final question is discussed with the entire group. Answers are written on a board or flip chart.

**55**

**Humorous drawings provide food for thought**

**56**

**Silly applications inject humor into interview skills sessions**

Altered application forms instantly inject humor and help break the ice in classes given by Patti Bee, a training officer at DSS Training in Oallands RD, Marion, Australia.

Bee hands out a two-page "training course application form" to each trainee, then leaves the room. On the front page, the application asks a series of serious questions about work experience, course expectations, etc. On the second page the questions become increasingly personal or silly, asking the color of people's underwear and what they ate for breakfast.

Bee returns when she hears participants snickering and talking about the applications. She asks participants to introduce themselves and answer one question from the silly side of the form. And finally, she discusses what the participants want from the course.

**57**

**Stressing potential of trainees sets the stage for training**

Maria Howard of Ensco Inc. strives to provide a motivational environment for participants before her seminars start. Part of Howard's managerial responsibility involves suggesting seminars for employees, depending on areas of growth needed. When she discusses proposed sessions with employees, she tries to make them feel they were chosen because they have special potential, rather than a skill deficiency. That nuance helps start each participant off with a more positive attitude.

Howard also attends seminars as a co-participant with some of those she manages. She chooses seminars of interest to her that also fit with the employee's duties. Not only does the employee feel hand-picked, Howard says, but the strategy also builds a sense of teamwork.

## 58

**'Gift-giving' exercise promotes bonding**

Linda Fagen uses the "gift-giving" activity to promote bonding among her staff members and to generate positive feedback between trainees during team-building sessions. At the end of her sessions, Fagen gives each participant a piece of paper to tear into two pieces. She tells participants to write one something-money-can't-buy intangible gift for the two trainees sitting on either side of them. Some examples of "gifts" are: You have a nice smile, you have a good sense of humor, you are enjoyable to work with, or you are a good team player, helpful, or professional. Each person gives two "gifts" and receives two gifts from the trainees on either side of them. After the exchange, Fagen asks the group if everyone got their gifts and checks to see if everyone liked them.

**59**

**Visual helps participants identify dangerous stress levels**

To remind participants they need to closely monitor their stress levels on the job and take the steps to ease unhealthy levels, Cecelia Soares, owner of Viewpoint Consultation in Walnut Creek, CA, asks for a volunteer to come to the front of the class and name all of the potential "stressors" faced on the job.

For each stressor named, she hands the volunteer an eight-ounce Styrofoam or paper cup to hold. Stacking them is not allowed. Eventually, as the volunteer begins to juggle more cups, the cups begin to fall. Soares says it's a good visual demonstration of "employees being unable to handle an unlimited amount of anything, particularly stress."

She tweaks the exercise by having the volunteer stand on one foot, or with one hand tied behind his or her back, while holding the cups. "That illustrates what happens if you're really stressed and one more stressor comes to push you over the edge," she says.

# 60

## Hula Hoop activity underscores benefits of teamwork

A Hula Hoop doubles as a fun and effective teaching tool for participants in Jack Norwood's classes. Norwood says this activity — which is based on an old party game — helps get a class loosened up and better acquainted, while building teamwork among participants.

Norwood, internal organizational developmental consultant with US West, Denver, has the class form a circle and hold hands, then places a Hula Hoop somewhere in the circle so that two people are holding hands through the hoop. He asks group members to estimate how long they think it will take to get the hoop around the circle — without letting go of hands. He says the group usually estimates much longer than it actually takes. Following the activity, Norwood discusses goal setting and how the group's perception of what they thought they could achieve was less than what they actually achieved. He reminds the group not to downplay their abilities to succeed when setting goals — as a team and individually.

Norwood then places a second smaller hoop at the opposite side of the circle and tells the group that the hoops must go around the circle in opposite directions without anyone in the group letting go of hands. He has the group determine how much time they think the activity will take. Once again, they usually overestimate the time it actually takes to complete the activity.

After the activity, he debriefs the group on their success in working together as a team, pointing out how positive encouragement from other team members and good communication helped move the hoop through the circle faster.

# 61

**Stress scenarios build group spirit**

Nancy Hensel, a consultant from Safety Harbor, FL, begins a training session on stress with all participants collaborating on a hypothetical stressful day. She begins by saying something like, "My alarm doesn't go off," and then participant number one adds, "And I'm 35 minutes late for an appointment with the company president," and person number two adds something else, and so on until each person has contributed something. The resulting scenario is a more stressful day than anyone could probably live through, which makes the topic of coping with stress that much easier.

The same concept could be applied to other types of training. Using the exercise for "worst day as a manager," or "worst day as a salesperson" are just two adaptations that could start a spirited discussion of job-related problems and build group spirit.

# Chapter Four Tips:
# Puzzles & Games

## 62

**Simple crosswords enhance attendee mix**

This ice breaker is tailored toward getting table members (five to seven people at a table) better acquainted.

Give each table leader or each participant a sheet with crossword puzzle-like clues. Allow the groups at each table three minutes to get as many answers as they can. You can preface the ice breaker by either saying all of these answers have answers have something in common, or you can take the hint a step further by saying they all end with the letters "go."

Here are the quiz questions:

1. City where the "fog creeps in on little cat feet."
2. Government order that stops trade.
3. A Beatle.
4. Cartoon character who said, "We have met the enemy and they is us."
5. Zodiac sign.
6. A shade of blue.
7. Spanish for friend.
8. Dance where "it takes two."
9. Zaire's old name.
10. Tropical fruit.
11. Freighters carry this.
12. James Stewart starred in this 1958 Hitchcock thriller.
13. City in North Dakota.
14. Lower back rheumatism.

15. Gulag _____.
16. Cuban drum.
17. Port in Samoa
18. Author of *Les Miserables*.
19. Stick you bounce up and down on.
20. Popular board game.
21. Freud's term for conscience.
22. Pink tropical bird.
23. $200 if you pass this.

Answers: 1. Chicago. 2. Embargo. 3. Ringo. 4. Pogo. 5. Virgo. 6. Indigo. 7. Amigo. 8. Tango. 9. Congo. 10. Mango. 11. Cargo. 12. Vertigo. 13. Fargo. 14. Lumbago. 15. Archipelago. 16. Bongo. 17. Pago Pago. 18. Victor Hugo. 19. Pogo. 20. Stratego. 21. Ego. 22. Flamingo. 23. Go.

# 63

## Activity, Discussion, Application approach makes exercises useful

It's easy to schedule activities that are fun, interesting, or exciting. But trainers then run the risk of criticism because those activities aren't practical, relevant, or useful. The Activity, Discussion, Application approach can eliminate that problem. The steps are simple: Do an activity, then make an application to the real world.

For example, reward people throughout the first day by giving them a potato. At the end of the day, give them the choice of either coming up and doing an activity or of giving the potato to someone else and letting them do it.

Then have them come up in front of the group, and give them soda straws. Ask them and the non-participants whether they believe you can tell them how to put the straws through the potatoes — with a single blow so that each participant can accomplish the task. After asking for a show of hands, ask how many believe strongly enough that they'd bet $100. Most hands drop.

Then show the participants how to do the task. After several tries all of them get the straw through the potato. The key to success is covering the air hole in the straw and, perhaps most importantly, following through.

Next discuss the activity — did they have to believe they could do it, or simply believe enough that they were willing to try? How did they feel being up front? How did observers feel about being observers, rather than participants? How important was follow-through?

Finally there's application in the real world: Ideas mean nothing without follow-through, and they don't have to believe they'll all work — just believe enough so they're willing to try an idea or two and then follow through.

**64**

**Creative problem-solving requires new perspectives**

The next time you want to put a different spin on a tired exercise, consider the approach of trainer Tony Manning. Give participants a single sheet of paper and ask them to make a plane that flies. Each person will more than likely be successful and also be able to demonstrate if any are having problems. Next ask that they use a fresh sheet of paper to create a new flying machine. Allow them the same amount of time to look for an entirely new design — a revolutionary new airborne machine that must fly.

In all likelihood, very few will succeed. Most will build upon or slightly alter the conventional design. When all have finished, take a piece of paper, crush it into a ball and throw it across the room. Explain that the problem was to create a new flying machine, not to repeat more of the same. A ball of paper will fly. It doesn't matter whether something fits our concept. What is critical is whether that it fits the parameters of the individual problem — or the valid requirements of the participant's customer or client.

**C**hris King, a consultant in Cleveland, OH, prepares a handout listing various types of human characteristics. As an opener, participants circulate to find people that fit every description, in the process making contact with most others in the class. Here's a short list of possibilities:

Voluntary morning person, involuntary morning person, risk taker, do-it-now person, do-it-later person, organized person, slightly disorganized person, really disorganized person, creative person, artistic person, health-food person, exercise person, fast driver, careful driver...

**65**

**Opener starts group quickly, enhances mingling**

**66**

**Simple, fun activities aid name recall**

Debra Gillman, patient education coordinator at St. Luke's Medical Center, Milwaukee, WI, breaks the ice with her participants by asking people to share their middle initials and having others in the group try to guess what they stand for. It gets people acquainted quickly and helps them remember names.

■ Vonda Ramey-Garrison, senior college relations administrator, Ashland Chemical Inc., Columbus, OH, has all participants remove their shoes and throw them in a pile in the middle of the room. Each person is then asked to pick someone else's shoes from the pile. The idea is to match the shoes with the correct owner, and get to know your fellow participants along the way.

**P**articipants are challenged to think creatively, and also to make "true confessions" during this ice breaker recommended by Lori Preston, training specialist at Electronic Data Systems.

Start by giving each participant 10 toothpicks or other counters. Then ask the first participant to talk about something they have never done, for example, "I've never jaywalked." After the statement, anyone in the group who has jaywalked has to forfeit a toothpick to the kitty. Then the next person shares one thing he or she has never done, and again anyone who has done it loses a toothpick. The disclosures continue around the room until someone has lost all 10 toothpicks. It's an entertaining way for people to get to know one another both by the things they have done, and the things they haven't done.

**67**

**'True confessions' game entertains, acquaints learners**

**68**

**Acrostics enhance review of course topics**

An "acrostic" challenge can help participants creatively review course content. For example, if your course deals with customer relations, put the letters CUSTOMER RELATIONS vertically on a flip chart and ask the participants to come up with learning points that start with each of those letters.

**A** progressive introduction game, with a focus on the class topic, is the opener preferred by Marsha Corbett, senior training consultant for Kaset Inc. If the group is sales-oriented, for example, the first person might say, "I'm Mary and persistence makes me effective in sales." Then the second person adds, "I'm Joe and product knowledge makes me effective in sales, and persistence makes Mary effective." This continues as each person introduces himself or herself and everyone who preceded. The first person concludes by reintroducing all of the others.

**69**

**Introduction game provides topic tie-in**

**Puzzler is food for thought after a break**

Here is quick exercise you can prepare on an overhead transparency and project near the end of a coffee break. It helps people refocus their attention to the front of the room and make the transition back to the program.

> Luke had it before.
> Paul had it behind.
> Matthew never had it at all.
> All girls have it once;
> boys can not have it.
> Old Mr. Mulligan had it,
> twice in succession.
> Dr. Lowell had it before and
> behind; he had it twice as
> bad behind as before.

The answer is the letter "L."

Alice Szepietowski, a New Jersey consultant, uses a variation on human bingo at the beginning of her training programs to get people involved. Before the program begins, she asks participants some personal information: size of their families, hometowns, hobbies, jobs they've had with the company, etc.

She then hands participants a sheet with blocks containing clues about others in the seminar. As they find the individual who matches the clues, that person initials the block. No repeats are permitted on any sheet. The questioning required to find the people who match the clues helps participants get acquainted.

**71**

**Human bingo promotes participant involvement**

**72**

**Nonsense game reinforces course terminology**

Kevin Blanding, a district psychologist with Morongo Unified School District in California, uses a variation on the game "Balderdash" to introduce or review course definitions.

The players write down what they think a concept means and then their answers are shuffled with the right definition and read aloud. Each team then tries to guess the correct answer. Blanding says the game makes for a humorous session that reinforces proper use of terminology.

**T**raining in product knowledge is critical to many jobs, but often doesn't rate high on the fun meter. At Commonwealth Federal Savings & Loan, training specialist Kathi Rees designs her training programs keeping in mind the belief that learning is directly proportional to the amount of fun participants have.

She titles one class, "Savings & Known: The Banking Knowledge Game." After about two and a half hours of the workshop, she brings out "The Products & Services Game," which she modeled after the popular "Trivial Pursuit" game. The six categories she uses are consistent with the game board: checking accounts, savings accounts, certificate of deposits, etc. Rees says the game has proven to be a popular and effective method of making a dry training topic fun.

# 73

**'Trivial Pursuit' format aids in product training**

**74**

**Glasses, puzzles make fun exercise props**

Peggy Bennett, northern region trainer for The Pantry, uses children's puzzles to help participants understand the significance of clear and specific instructions.

Bennett has a volunteer wear a set of safety glasses with the lenses painted black, so he or she can't see. The trainer then hands a child's puzzle tray with about 12 to 15 pieces to the participant and verbally explains the instructions needed to complete the puzzle. Once the puzzle is constructed the trainer and the volunteer discuss their feelings, frustrations, and tips for better communication.

**P**air up participants for an introductory ice breaker with an "Old Maid" card game. Cheryl Hebdon, instructor with US West Communications in Lakewood, CO, tapes pairs of cards face down or under the tables where participants sit. Participants look at their cards and circulate around the room, introducing themselves and asking questions to locate their partner cards without telling others what cards they hold.

**75**

**Old Maid card game speeds learner introductions**

# 76

**Domino exercise enhances listening skills**

Liz Hebert, a trainer with Waste Management of Oak Brook, IL, offers this technique for sales training in interpersonal communication skills:

Break participants into groups of three. Give each group eight dominos. Seat the participants so one person in each group faces away from the others. Have one of the other two arrange four dominos on a table; then have the other describe the layout as the third tries to duplicate it, without asking questions to clarify the directions.

Hebert then allows participants to switch positions and try again. Future rounds allow two-way communication between the participants. In very large groups or when time is short, Hebert says the exercise can be completed by one small group on an overhead projector while the rest observe.

**B**arbara Taraskiewicz, training coordinator for Kalamazoo Valley Community College, uses the common brainteaser pictures of the chalice/profiles and the old woman/young woman (below) for an introductory exercise that emphasizes the importance of focus and perception.

Rather than challenging participants to tell her what they see, she helps participants see both images and then points out that what they see first depends upon their focus of attention. She makes the point that we are prisoners of our perceptions and tend to only see what we're focused on, and that once we're focused, it becomes difficult to see other things that were there all along.

**77**

**Brainteasers help break bonds of limited perception**

**78**

**Tennis ball activity teaches participant names quickly**

Members of a group learn one another's names quickly with this exercise, says Judy Clarke, a training officer for American Express, Australia:

Participants stand in a circle. The instructor states her name and tosses a tennis ball to a student. That person, in turn, says his name and tosses the ball to another. This continues until everyone has had the ball several times.

Then the rules change. As players toss the ball, they say the recipients' names instead of their own. The game always provides a few laughs while helping students and teacher alike to learn participants' names.

**Human scavenger hunt encourages dialogue**

Dale Ditmanson, training specialist for the National Park Service, asks each participant to send in an "autobiography" before the course. As an ice breaker, he selects a line or two from each autobiography and types them as a list.

Participants are given the list as they arrive, then sent out on a "human scavenger hunt" in the classroom until they uncover which person matches each line on the sheet.

## 80

## 'Four corners' game mixes participants

Mary Ellen Burchell, outdoor program director for the Michigan Trails Girl Scout Council, likes to use the "Forced Choices" or "Four Corners" activity as a way to get people acquainted. It's also used to discover participants' common interests, needs, or experiences.

Burchell makes four flip-chart pages with four different descriptive words or phrases on each page. For example, the first page might read "music, reading, athletics, and gourmet cooking." Participants choose one and then go to the corner of the room assigned to that phrase and have a one-minute discussion on why they made that choice. Then one person reports to the entire group some of the reasons their group made that choice. The next page is flipped into view and people make new choices until all four pages are used.

**E**ric Frederick, director of linen services, Aurora Health Care, opens some of his training programs with a round of introductions. He instructs the first person to say his or her name and provide one piece of personal information. The second in line then follows with his or her name, adds a bit of information, and repeats the information about the first person. Each person continues the process, repeating the information about all of the previous participants. The group helps out any time someone gets stuck. This works well with groups of up to 20 people, and helps people learn quite a bit about others in the group very quickly.

**81**

Name game fosters small-group learning

# Chapter Five Tips: Creative Resources

**82**

**Twine indicates effect of one person's actions on others**

In any session where demonstrating the effect one person's actions has upon others, such as team-building or leadership courses, Becky Schaefer, a manager of employee involvement at US West, Denver, uses the following exercise:

She divides students into groups of four to 10, depending on the size of the class. One person in each group is given a ball of twine. That person holds onto the end and passes the ball to another team member, and so on, until everyone in the small group is holding the strand at some point — keeping it taut without breaking it. Participants are encouraged to loop the twine around a person or two in the group to further complicate the equation, returning the ball to the first person to complete the circuit after all are connected.

The teams are then asked to experiment with movement. What happens when one person moves her hand to the left two feet? What happens if someone sits down? What sort of cooperation is necessary for the group to move across the room — all the while adhering to the objective of keeping the string taut without breaking it.

After several minutes, Schaefer asks what was learned. Did the string ever break? If so, why? Were some people forceful while others were accommodating? Did leaders develop? Too many of them? What kinds of communication worked? What didn't?

The main point, she says, is to demonstrate that every action a team member makes, no matter how insignificant it may seem, has an effect on others.

# 83

## Illustrating conflict resolution concepts drives point home

Using a simple demonstration makes a concept crystal clear to participants in T.J. Titcomb's team-building/conflict resolution classes.

Titcomb, director of training at Family Service, Lancaster, PA, begins the class with a discussion on the need to change expectations about conflict. Rather than assuming conflict is only negative, she strives to teach participants to see it as a motivator for change and a tool to ensure all major viewpoints are considered. Titcomb sets up these supplies at the front of the class: three transparent glass beakers or test tubes filled with water, small packets of sugar and salt, and colored glass marbles. She then demonstrates the difference between "soluble" (solvable) conflicts and "insoluble" (unsolvable) conflicts.

"Any conflict," she explains, "has two distinct viewpoints. Some conflicts are 'soluble.' The two parts combine, they don't disappear — they become something new, keeping the best of both." (She pours a small amount of sugar into a beaker of water and shakes it.)

"Some conflicts are sweet because they are easily resolved through collaboration." (She pours a small amount of salt into the second beaker of water and shakes it.)

"Other conflicts add spice to life. They are a little harder and take more effort to resolve. In time they may reappear again as the two parts separate. We may have to return later and work at them again to keep them soluble." (She shakes the beaker a second time.)

(She then holds up the third water beaker, drops in a glass marble, and shakes it.) "But we must also recognize that some conflicts cannot be resolved. What can we do when faced with insoluble conflicts? They can be understood, appreciated, and accepted. We step back and admire the diversity of ideas, opinions, and values among human beings. We learn that different is OK. We also decide as individuals when to stop trying to force solutions onto insoluble conflicts. We are then free to put our energy into changing our reaction to people and situations."

Titcomb gives each participant a marble as a reminder of the class.

# 84

## Lego exercise improves listening skills

To help improve communication skills and raise consciousness about treating customers with empathy, Andy Oman, training and development administrator for Hoffman Engineering, Anoka, MN, uses an exercise featuring a blindfold and Lego toys.

He first has his entire class study a preconstructed Lego model, often in the form of a plane or house, for one minute. Then one participant in a group of five to seven is blindfolded while other members disassemble the model. Using a photo of the model as a reference, group members instruct the blindfolded participant in reconstructing the model. Rules include no handing of pieces to the blindfolded member. Typical commands include things such as, "feel for the two-inch-wide tile and place at the far left corner." Oman usually provides two to four minutes for assembly.

Oman makes the point that new levels of understanding and communication skills are necessary for dealing with internal and external customers.

At the end of each day in Tom Stiers' multiday sessions, participants get a chance to address any "hanging issues" not aptly addressed during a course segment. Stiers, a training manager with 3M Co., Maplewood, MN, posts a flip chart featuring a large hangman's noose at the front of the class. He asks participants to jot any pertinent issues not addressed or questions left unanswered on Post-it Notes and to put them on the chart. The "hanging issues" are addressed by Stiers and through group discussion at the beginning of the next day's session, or as a closing activity at the end of each day.

**85**

**Open flip-chart lets learners address 'hanging issues'**

**86**

**Balloons add panache to sessions**

Balloons can add an eye-catching change and sense of adventure to your seminars. A batch of balloons can be used to choose topics or questions for discussion.

First, prepare a series of questions you want participants to discuss. Put the questions on small slips of paper and insert them in balloons before you blow them up. At the appropriate time, each group or individual chooses a balloon to pop. Inside they find the question they are supposed to discuss. As an alternative, the question could be one you want the whole group to answer, or a presentation you want them to prepare. You may also want to use the color of balloon to designate the degree of question difficulty.

**T**oys are a staple in most training rooms. To challenge participants to think creatively and work smarter, Pam Wooldridge, a training specialist for Strouds, enlists the help of a toy easily found in most stores: a paddle with a ball attached to it by a rubber string.

At the end of a day or an individual learning unit, she asks for a volunteer to review a set of points made in class while keeping the ball in motion (those are her exact instructions). Most try to bounce the ball against the paddle, but soon realize that Wooldridge's only stipulation was to keep the ball moving. Soon, she says, participants are swinging the ball until it is wrapped around the paddle or making it sway back and forth like a pendulum.

After the review, Wooldridge makes the point that the exercise shows that people often try to make a task more difficult than it needs to be, and that by thinking creatively they can come up with better ways of doing things.

Note: The exercise can also be used as a session opener or energizer, with participants instructed to keep the ball in motion while they introduce themselves.

**87**

**Paddle ball exercise teaches learners to think more creatively**

**88**

**Music enriches learning process, aids retention**

Music can set a mood to learn by. Consider making available to participants a varied selection of tapes they can listen to during breaks. You don't need anything too formal — just tapes, an uncomplicated and reliable tape player, and easy access so participants can handle the details themselves. Be sure you allow people the freedom to indicate when the music is bothersome as well.

Plan also to use the music during individual or group activities. Music such as Vivaldi's *Four Seasons* or Steven Halpern's *Spectrum Suite* can help to create an environment conducive to learning. Music can also be used to promote and reinforce course content. For one class, Harriet Reichman at Citibank sent her participants a tape before classes began with an upbeat introduction to her program. Then she had a professional singer record (with an upbeat popular tune) selected key ideas covered in training to follow-up and reinforce the training. The follow-up tape was sent to participants about a week after the training program ended.

**89**

**Jumpstart group with a quick brainteaser**

# H

ere's a quick puzzler you can use after lunch or a break. Place these numbers on a flip chart or whiteboard:

8, 11, 15, 5, 14, 1, 7,
6, 10, 13, 3, 12, 2

Tell the audience, "You're seeing all the numbers from one to 15 with the exception of four and nine. Your task is to decide why the numbers are arranged in this sequence, then put the missing numbers in their proper places."

Take the test yourself right now. After you've made your decision, turn this page upside down for the correct answer.

Answer: The numbers are listed alphabetically. Therefore, four goes after five and nine follows 14.

**90**

**Bells and chimes serve well as feedback devices**

Toys that emit sounds like a bomb dropping, a laser discharging, or a machine gun firing are great for eliciting group feedback. Eileen McDargh of McDargh Communications, Laguna Niguel, CA, says that bells, whistles, chimes, gongs, and even clackers serve just as well in group feedback exercises — and help "get Rambo out of the classroom" at the same time.

When it is time for review, Debra Gillman, patient education coordinator at St. Luke's Medical Center, Milwaukee, WI, has participants throw a Nerf ball or Koosh ball back and forth. As each person catches the ball, he or she has to mention a learning point or concept heard in the class, then toss the ball to another person. It is permissible to repeat something that someone else has said, if it's stated in different words.

**91**

**Tossing a Koosh ball creates an active review**

**92**

**Creative props personalize a subject**

Creative props can often pique people's curiosity and get them involved in what appears to be a difficult or unpleasant topic. Bill Beale, income assistance coordinator for the State of Washington in Seattle, trains employees on how to help clients select good child care so employees understand the importance of that task as part of their jobs.

Beale gives the participants teddy bears with blank name tags on them. Participants are asked to give their bears the name of a child who is important to them. The class discussion then centers around what is important in day care for their bear/child. It personalizes the subject, emphasizes that they already know a great deal about child care, and allows participants to share individual knowledge. It makes the learning process fun as well as more meaningful for groups that are resistant to adding this new aspect to their client interviews.

**P**otential reward items are often found in unexpected places. A little creative thinking about commonplace items can keep you well-stocked with rewards.

One trainer found complimentary books of matches at the reception of a motor speedway club with the slogan: "Where winners come together." The club donated a few dozen to be used in varied training sessions.

Check a stationery or paper party products store for items that say "Congratulations" or "Thank You" that could be tied to training themes.

A trip to the local liquidator or outlet store may also yield a variety of inexpensive pens, paperweights, and calendars with slogans extolling teamwork or quality. Although items from those sources often have company names imprinted, the unrelated business names keep the "award" lighthearted.

**93**

**Gather reward items from unusual places**

**94**

**Newspaper format captures attendee imagination**

Trainer Becky Grupa uses a tried-and-true communication vehicle — the newspaper — to highlight substantial changes in a system of making payments on insurance claims at Principal Financial Group in Minneapolis.

Not only does she publish the information in newspaper style, she bundles her handouts individually and stuffs them into a carrier's bag. At the start of her training sessions she throws a paper to each participant and shouts, "Extra, extra, read all about it." The news is always well-received, she says.

At the beginning of her workshops, Mary Beth Brunke, training coordinator for Household International, gives each participant an envelope not to be opened until the end of the program.

Participants aren't told what is in the envelopes, just that they have value and it is important they hold onto them. Inside is a certificate of achievement, a pocket-size reference book, and other items relevant to the course.

Trainees set expectations that something important is inside. The contents give them some positive "strokes" for their accomplishments and reinforce the value of using what they've learned.

As a variation of this exercise, Brunke has participants play "20 Questions." Attendees are allowed to ask questions about the items sealed in the envelope. Only yes and no questions may be asked, and the participants may use one of their turns to guess the contents at any time.

**95**

**Sealed envelope gimmick piques participant interest**

**96**

**Dots as reference markers ease recall**

Red stick-on dots, such as those used to code file folders, can be used to mark places in workbooks and identify meaningful material. Kevin Griffiths, director of KRG Consultants, provides strips of dots at each table so that as participants come across key points, they can place a color dot in the margin.

It makes it easy, Griffiths says, for participants to later scan the workbook and pick out ideas they can use for action planning.

**97**

**Baby photos are great peer equalizers**

Using participants' baby photos can help break the ice and drive home some learning points, according to Lisa Monopoli of National Car Rental System. She has participants send a baby photo prior to the seminar. She numbers and displays the baby pictures, and has participants match them up by voting on who's who. When the votes are tallied everyone has a good laugh, she says. Monopoli says this activity is especially effective for a seminar that combines work peers of different professional levels.

Monopoli says that aside from being fun, the opener helps make two points:

• When conducting a class with participants who are of different professional levels, the activity helps break the ice by pointing out that we all started out on the same level.

• When conducting courses where change is being introduced, it helps to demonstrate how much change each of us has already been through and that change is inevitable.

**98**

**Blank wall allows trainees to voice concerns**

Participants share their thoughts on a large roll of paper, such as butcher paper or newsprint, taped across a wall in classes taught by Dennis Link, operations training coordinator for Amoco Oil in Texas City, TX. He divides the paper into three sections labeled: Issues/Concerns, Main Ideas, and Thoughts/Feelings. Link encourages people to express themselves on the wall. The process helps others to learn and to remember key points on the wall. He says it is a tremendous way to keep trainees involved in training.

**P**eople often are unaware of how they "beat up on themselves" during a session, says Patti Lovaas, by doing things like apologizing for their answer to a question, by saying things like, "I'm no expert but..." before offering input, or by saying they don't have enough experience to contribute meaningfully.

To make people aware of that behavior, Lovaas, a training specialist for the Social Security Administration, Denver, brings a whip to class (a wooden dowel with colorful strips of plastic attached to one end). She assigns someone to be the "keeper of the whip." When that person hears anyone in the room saying or implying derogatory things about themselves or anyone else, the keeper passes the whip to the offender, as a reminder of the "beating" that person is dishing out. Lovaas got her "whip" from a magic store. Most craft stores carry the items necessary to make one.

**99**

**Prop helps 'whip' attitudes into shape**

**'Wanted' posters provide fun, enhance session**

Students in training courses conducted by Craig Hauser and Dale Morehouse, both in training and development at Walt Disney World, Orlando, FL, get to know one another via "wanted" posters. Upon arrival, attendees are given a sheet with two empty boxes at the top for front and profile mug shots, and a number of blanks below, labeled "background" (for information about family, place of birth, career information), and "known behaviors" (for information about hobbies). Other points of interest may also be included to add flavor to the posters, such as "car last seen in" or "known to watch the following television programs."

The trainer tapes the posters to a wall. At the bottom of each sheet are a number of blanks. Participants are asked to read the posters and mark at the bottom of each one whom they think it describes.

The trainer, meanwhile, asks each participant to pose for two Polaroid photos, preferably out of sight of the rest of the class. The shots are taken against the backdrop of a height marker similar to those shown in actual mug shots. Instead of holding a serial number, participants create tagboard signs displaying their first names and any "known alias," for example, "Nancy a.k.a. The Accountant."

After everyone has had photos taken and had a chance to guess whom the posters belong to, the instructor asks the students to tape their photos in the appropriate places on their posters.

## 101

**Simple pennants enrich learning setting**

Construction paper pennants reinforce the team attitude in classes facilitated by Leslie Mizerak.

Mizerak, a training facilitator at Southern State Community College in Wilmington, OH, posts large baseball-style pennants on classroom walls during courses involving workplace teams, labeled with team names and simple slogans. She provides smaller versions for people to wear on their shirts to identify which team students are from during mixed-group activities.

"It may sound childish," she says, "but it helps people feel real team spirit."

# About the Author...

**R**obert Pike has been developing and implementing training programs for business, industry, government, and the professions since 1969. As president of Creative Training Techniques International Inc., Resources for Organizations Inc., and The Resources Group Inc. based in Edina, MN, he leads over 150 sessions each year on topics such as leadership, attitudes, motivation, communication, decision-making, problem-solving, personal and organizational effectiveness, conflict management, team-building, and managerial productivity.

More than 50,000 trainers have attended Pike's Creative Training Techniques® workshops. As a consultant, he has worked with such organizations as American Express, Upjohn, Hallmark Cards Inc., IBM, PSE&G, Bally's Casino Resort, and Shell Oil. A member of the American Society for Training and Development (ASTD) since 1972, he has served on three of the organization's national design groups, and held office as director of special interest groups and as a member of the national board.

An outstanding speaker, Pike has been a presenter at regional and national conferences for ASTD and other organizations. He currently serves as co-chairman of the Professional Emphasis Groups for the National Speakers' Association. He was recently granted the professional designation of Certified Speaking Professional (CSP) by the NSA, an endorsement earned by only 170 of the organization's 3,800 members.

Pike is editor of Lakewood Publications' *Creative Training Techniques* newsletter, author of *The Creative Training Techniques Handbook*, and has contributed articles to *TRAINING Magazine*, *The Personnel Administrator*, and *Self-Development Journal*. He has been listed, since 1980, in *Who's Who in the Midwest* and is listed in *Who's Who in Finance and Industry*.

## Want More Copies?

This and most other Lakewood books are available at special quantity discounts when purchased in bulk. For details write Lakewood Books, 50 South Ninth Street, Minneapolis, MN 55402. Call (800) 707-7769 or (612) 333-0471. Or fax (612) 340-4819. Visit our web page at www.lakewoodpub.com.

## More on Training

Powerful Audiovisual Techniques: 101 Ideas to Increase the Impact and Effectiveness of Your Training $14.95

Dynamic Openers & Energizers: 101 Tips and Tactics for Enlivening Your Training Classroom $14.95

Optimizing Training Transfer: 101 Techniques for Improving Training Retention and Application $14.95

Managing the Front-End of Training: 101 Ways to Analyze Training Needs — And Get Results! $14.95

Motivating Your Trainees: 101 Proven Ways to Get Them to Really Want to Learn $14.95

Creative Training Techniques Handbook: Tips, Tactics, and How-To's for Delivering Effective Training, 2nd Edition $49.95

Creative Training Techniques Newsletter: Tips, Tactics, and How-To's for Delivering Effective Training $ 99/12 issues